Whispers, Secrets and Promises

Whispers, Secrets and Promises

E. Ethelbert Miller

DuForcelf

Whispers, Secrets and Promises

Founded in 1978, Black Classic Press specializes in bringing to light obscure and significant works by and about people of African descent. If our books are not available in your area, ask your local bookseller to order them. Our current list of titles can be obtained by writing:

Black Classic Press
c/o List
P.O. Box 13414
Baltimore, MD 21203

A Young Press With Some Very Old Ideas

Printed by BCP Digital Printing

**To live is to build a ship and a harbor
at the same time.**

-Yehuda Amichai

I have heard that after thirty a man
wakes up sad every morning.

-Emerson

Preface

This is the first book I've written that I decided not to dedicate to anyone. I guess this is my book. The poems are a collection of things I needed to say. Throughout the work, one will discover the themes of despair, depression and desire. This book documents many failed relationships and broken promises. In many ways, this poetry collection closes a personal door in my life. As I move towards becoming fifty, *Whispers, Secrets and Promises* represents an entrance into what I now call my own Gethsemane.

Acknowledgments

Some of the poems in this collection have also been previously published in the following journals and anthologies:

The Carolina Quarterly
The Northwest Side Story
Route One
The American Voice
Callaloo
The Drumming Between Us
Tailwind
Crossroads: A Journal of Southern Culture
Prism
Crab Orchard Review
Gargoyle
River Oak Review
phati'tude
WordWrights
Body and Soul by rundu
Catch the Fire edited by Derrick I.M. Gilbert

A special thanks goes to Philana Griffin for reading and preparing the manuscript in collaboration with E. Ethelbert Miller.

Table of Contents

INTRODUCTION

As the story goes, the great Argentine man of letters Jorge Luis Borges had a singular desire to do one thing before he died: spend an afternoon on a bank of the Mississippi River, America's greatest life source. The nearly blind Borges, an ardent admirer of Mark Twain, wanted to feel the power of the river T. S. Eliot had dubbed "the Great Brown God." Eventually Borges found his way to Hannibal, Missouri, courtesy of a cabal of Twain scholars and distinguished East Coast *literati*. Upon being led to the great river's bank, the elegantly attired octogenarian shocked his hosts by plunging straight into the Mississippi—three-piece suit and all—without even removing his watch or wallet. It was as if Borges was baptizing himself in the river; when he returned dripping to dry land, the poet proclaimed, "Ah, at last, at last I understand America."

Encountering E. Ethelbert Miller's haunting, stripped-down, but complex poems in *Whispers, Secrets and Promises* (1998) is like wading neck-deep into the Mississippi River while dressed in your Sunday best. There is a calm integrity that runs through this introspective collection that is maintained even while the poet is rushed away in a swirling current of African American history, nostalgia, loneliness, and despair. The 48-year-old Miller, director of Howard University's African American Resource Center, is a recorder of lost emotions whose elegiac verse reveals the longing and confusion of the African diaspora. *Whispers, Secrets and Promises* is also an elegant volume of ironic but tenderhearted love poems in which the caress of a woman's breast or a couple's twilight frolic become divine spiritual moments. Not since Langston Hughes has an African American poet so ably combined the oral and literary traditions of his people to produce a collective poetic portrait of a singular Black man searching for love in a world gone awry. "I tried from the beginning to make my work accessible to both language and ideas," Miller once commented in *The Washington Review*. "In some ways I modeled myself after Langston Hughes—he was the writer who best embodied and articulated the hope and dreams of our people."

The beginning for Miller was the South Bronx, where he was born on November 20, 1950 to parents of West Indian ancestry. At the time, multiculturalism was not an academic approach but an everyday reality in which old men from Sicily swapped stories with Jamaican matriarchs as they waited in line at the delicatessen to buy gefilte fish from Russian Jews. Racism was apparent, and Caribbean American families like the Millers longed to embrace the American dream as defined by the Jim Crow-ruled Eisenhower era. For young Ethelbert, however, poetry was not to be found in mainstream anthologies but in the multilingual street talk of the South Bronx. "I went to Paul Laurence Dunbar Junior High School in New York, but nobody in my school was reading Dunbar," Miller remembers. "I didn't really get an appreciation for African-American literature until I attended Howard University. But I did pick up language on the streets."

Miller's emergence as a poet began in September 1968, when he made the jump from an integrated high school to Howard's all-Black campus. Dr. Martin Luther King, Jr., had been assassinated just five months earlier in Memphis, and the ghettos of Los Angeles and Detroit were smoldering with rage. Newark poet LeRoi Jones (Amiri Baraka) was pushing for the creation of African American studies departments at major universities and the Black Arts movement was flourishing across the nation. Just five months before Miller's arrival at Howard University, a student takeover had occurred, and fiery alumnus Stokely Carmichael—a Trinidadian whose manifesto *Black Power* (1967) was quoted on the quad like holy scripture— was a frequent presence on campus. James Brown's "Say It Loud: I'm Black and I'm Proud" blared from dormitory windows and blended with Jimi Hendrix's psychedelic rendition of the "Star Spangled Banner," proof that a Black artist had launched a guitar revolution.

But Miller kept his eyes trained on the poets. "Baraka was my hero because his voice actually triggered the Black Arts Movement, creating the transformative awareness and consciousness which is necessary for African-American culture to survive," he recalls. "I think there is a direct link between Baraka and Langston in terms of true artists who write in every genre: autobiography, short stories, plays, poems. Baraka is one of the major writers who has literally affected a generation." With Hughes and Baraka as inspiration, Miller started writing poems on the backs of envelopes and sending them to appreciative friends. A few of his verses appeared in Howard's newspaper *The Hilltop* in 1969–70, and others were read on the campus radio station to modest acclaim.

Upon graduating from Howard in 1972, Miller became attracted to the work of such Black Arts movement poets as Haki Madhubuti and Sonia Sanchez, avoiding the didactic diatribes of H. Rap Brown and Huey Newton. He was influenced instead by protest singers such as Phil Ochs and Bob Dylan, and he sought poetry in politics, art in his daily academic regimen. Although Miller fervently admired Malcolm X, he harbored no anti-White resentment courtesy of his South Bronx upbringing and believed he could learn more from William Carlos Williams's poetic minimalism than from Eldridge Cleaver's *Soul on Ice*.

Rather than point fingers at racist Whites in his poetry and politics, since the early 1970s, Miller has urged Black men to look at themselves, to celebrate the revelatory power of love while protesting against unjust social conditions. Miller found the long-winded rants of the Black Panthers futile, adhering instead to what South African poet Denis Brutus called "Economy of Words"—throwing unnecessary adjectives and overused clichés away and keeping only the pith. Like Irish playwright John Millington Synge, Miller believed that each word in a poem should burst with flavor like a nut or apple.

Miller emerged as a real presence on the Washington, DC poetry scene in the mid-1970s when he co-edited *Hoo Doo Magazine* with Ahmos Zu-Bolton II and edited *Synergy: An Anthology of Washington, D.C. Black Poetry* (1975). His first volume of poetry, *Andromeda* (1974), received warm accolades, with critics praising Miller for his highly developed sense of irony and irreverent wit. Appointed director of the African American Resource Center at Howard University in 1974, Miller began organizing public poetry readings throughout Washington, DC, and he initiated the Ascension Series, which provided an open mike for talented young versemakers. "He's a mover, shaker, organizer, encourager, and scolder," noted Henry Taylor, the Pulitzer Prize-winning poet who heads American University's creative writing program.

Most of Washington, DC's cultural elite grew enamored of Miller as Howard University's African American literary archivist and creative writing teacher. But while he promoted the poetry of others, he remained shy about his own. In recognition of Miller's success at building such a literary community, DC Mayor Marion Barry, Jr., proclaimed September 28, 1979, "E. Ethelbert Miller Day," and in 1982 gave him the Mayor's Art Award for Literature. In coming years, the awards would keep coming, including the 1995 O.B. Hardison, Jr. Poetry Prize and an honorary doctorate in literature from Emory & Henry College in 1996.

Miller explores gender in a sensitive way that most male African American poets have avoided. With the publication of *Where Are the Love Poems For Dictators?* (1986), inspired by a journey to Central America, Miller successfully melded African American traditions and sentiments with those of Latinos, feminists, Asian Americans, and gays and lesbians, and he developed an unwavering sympathy for Nicaragua's leftist Sandinistas. June Jordan thereafter became one of his most steadfast champions, having written an appreciative introduction to Miller's *Season of Hunger/Cry of Rain, Poems: 1975–1980* (1982), while the legendary Gwendolyn Brooks deemed him "one of the most significant and influential poets of our time." These stunning tributes helped establish the mild-mannered thinker from the South Bronx, who had learned to roam the world like Langston Hughes, as one of the most respected poets of his generation.

Which brings us to the extraordinary matter at hand: *Whispers, Secrets and Promises*. First the reader encounters the disclaimer that this collection, brimming with transcendental new love poems from the

1980s and 1990s, is not dedicated to any specific person. "I started dedicating a lot of love poems," Miller jokes, "and I learned not to do that anymore." There is no simple way to describe the beautiful simplicity, haunting soulfulness, and dreamy surrealism of such works as "A House In Provincetown" and "Lover Behind a Blue Door." These are not "Black poems" but universal cries of longing that will stagger even the most casual reader. Miller's laments are in words as evocative as the paintings of Edward Hopper or the photographs of Walker Evans.

America's roots music also echoes throughout *Whispers, Secrets and Promises* with its tumultuous and joyous forbears appearing through muted grace notes in the background in most of the poems: Big Mama Thornton singing the all-night blues in a Houston juke joint, Tommy Dorsey composing "Precious Lord" some faded and forgotten morning, Buddy Bolden blowing his crazy jazz in a Storyville brothel that has long since disappeared. A particularly ethereal favorite of mine is "The Voice of Aretha Franklin Surprises Me," which shows that like so many other African American greats—Malcolm X, James Baldwin, Richard Wright—Miller had to leave America to fully recognize the beauty of his own Black heritage. Listening to Aretha Franklin on the radio at dusk in a Muslim country as a Sahara wind blew into his hotel bedroom engulfed Miller with a newly profound sense of the American experience as surely as the Mississippi River current that had pushed so vigorously against Borges' delicate old legs.

But race itself sounds only a grace note in *Whispers, Secrets and Promises*. These evocative poems are universal in sentiment, dealing with family squabbles, health concerns, and the love of parents. Poignant images abound from Miller's youth, of his weary father shaving and his aging mother announcing that Aunt Gwen has died. Miller has a genius for finding the profundity in such commonplaces like William Wordsworth's "spots of time" or Jean-Paul Sartre's "perfect moments." We all know these frozen moments: I once eyed a poster in a Paris café of a photograph of Langston Hughes in Harlem, bearing the quote "The Sweet Flypaper of Life" on the bottom. I remember little else about my months in Paris, but the sight of that poster on a rainy night at a desolate café on the Left Bank at midnight will haunt me forever. Miller conjures up that feeling, that suspension in time, throughout *Whispers, Secrets and Promises*. Take, for example, the heart-breaking "I've Been Waiting For A Letter From You":

> *The wind blows a newspaper down the street*
> *Four boys bounce a ball on the gray sidewalk*
> *It's Friday afternoon and school is out*
> *The mailman stops and opens the mailbox*
> *I've been waiting for a letter from you.*

We've all known the ache of waiting for love that never comes, and Miller makes us relive the pain, dig up the moments buried within, and confront their wayward ghosts because he believes that in them the essence of life is found. There is a certain masochism in Miller's poetry: he refuses to let us forget our hurt. And African Americans in particular cannot afford to simply forget the horrors of the Middle Passage, slavery's oily whip, or Louisiana's lynchings. But Miller also insists that African Americans remember the joy of Jackie Robinson's batting title and the charm of a forgotten Ray Charles song not currently available on CD. He is an emotional excavator of the past, a historical archivist to whom myth is as potent as fact and tall tales as indispensable as census data. And as a devoted African American scholar, he purposefully draws aesthetic inspiration from the raw voices and unheard aspirations of common folk, treating street people with the same dignity as learned scholars. Miller is thus a people's poet, a sensitive observer who finds delight in the way humanity struggles to find meaning in an absurd world. There is a sly humor to Miller, reminiscent of Hughes, and most obvious in "Oh Nigeria!" where the poet's alter ego Omar represents the changes in African American culture brought about by the flourishing of Islamic traditions.

One cannot discuss E. Ethelbert Miller without mentioning rain or the threat of it, which permeates this collection of poetic snapshots. More than anything else *Whispers, Secrets and Promises* is about surviving the various storms of life. But rain brings growth, and Miller has the gift of pointing that out, offering hope through lost love in moments of personal despair. The fact that love exists, these poems seem to say, means that it can be found again, and *that* is what keeps us lurching forward with hope and pride. Taken together, these poems call to mind what José Ortega y Gasset wrote in *Meditations on Quixote* (1911): "I am myself and what is around me, and if I do not save it, it shall not save me."

—Douglas Brinkley
Director of the Eisenhower Center for American Studies and Professor of History, University of New Orleans

Whispers, Secrets and Promises

afternoon
and your eyes walk
across the table into
my hands

this is the beginning
of confessions and faith
or how you braid your
hair

a metaphor
for things left
unsaid

there is no need for us
to see the moon tonight
or watch each other sleep
we are hooked at the hip
in spirit and matters of
the heart

this day is a moment
of grace
one moment in a life
of many

Ask Me Now

like Thelonius Monk

I record my love for you
and no one understands it

the complexity of my
declarations

the strange way
it makes you feel

Rain

The storm passes and I hear your voice,
the soft thunder of love flashes like
lightning between each cloud of breath
you take. What can I say that will make
it rain again?

Love Inside Your Triangle

I.

rain falling
I feel your
wetness
on my hands

II.

on my tongue
the
taste of your
secrets

III.

I wake up inside
your dream
your legs surrounding
my morning
rise

Miami in November

the storm is gone
only our hands survive
after high winds and destruction
when we attempt to kiss again
it is difficult to understand
why we are not always together
you have a boyfriend now
and the sky is clear
I must love you from a distance
when rain falls again
remember my heart as shelter
remember my love as home

Do nothin' till you hear from me

what did Ellington mean
when he said

"I love you madly"

his hands touching a
piano not made of flesh

Bringing Back the Draft

I suck your breasts
till your nipples
stand erect like two
small soldiers ready
to go to war

The Bath

perhaps it would
have been better
if I had seen you
bathing in a stream

your innocence
would forgive
my staring

now when I say
I love you
my words fall
like water from
your breasts

sunrise and the dew
leaves without a trace today
grass grows without you

heart on fire
I am alone and
burning

Meal

1 Man
1 Woman
2 Bowls of Soup
1 Piece of Bread

Love fills
2 spoons

Conversation

I told her . . .she had very nice hips.
She told me . . . I shouldn't be looking around
corners.

I said . . . I like to see where I'm going.

Conjure

this is how
I remember you
undressing in moonlight

this is
the kiss
that opened hands

this movement
so gentle

this

Blue Candles

so much
love
between
us

blue
candles

burning

passion
is such
a hot
fire

smoke
curling
into
flesh

the
tip
of your
tongue
melting
into
mine

the first time I saw your back
I knew I was in love
the back of you
the smooth space where a man
could place his hands
the two of them
tracing the path down
the steps of your spine

O(h)

like the second letter
in the word love
your lips shape the
air I breathe

River

let us meet
near the river
where a small
boat is waiting
to take us across

there is land
beneath your heart
your love is water

In a Time of Desire

in this time of desire
the world stops
there are no tomorrows
only this moment
when we touch
for the first time

today begins and ends
inside of you

sometimes I think of loving you
and it's strange
the nakedness of it
the moment when it comes to realization
but not necessarily fact
the lust of dreams
the memory of moments talking but not touching . . . .
. . . what if
desire was to walk into morning
and find us together

There Are Nights

there are nights
when I miss your tongue
and the other parts of
you that speak to me
in ways that have no words

the moon is your breast
glowing in my hand and I
discover a second one so
close to the first and I
am thankful that I have two
hands and you have two breasts
and why we were created this way
is so wonderful that I cannot
find the words . . .

so let me take your tongue
and place it in my mouth
and let us speak a common
language in the dark and
let us speak of loving and let us
never be silent when we have
so much to say

When a Man Loves a Woman

for 6 months
a man could be
seen in her window
one day she came
outside to show
the joy of her
company

we touched her
roundness and felt
her world move

Unemployment

u once said
that u could never
see yourself loving me
but now here u are
reaching down between my legs
saying it's hard times
saying your man left u
and u still gotta have
the basic things in life
well I say baby
u better get away
cause u need to learn
that u can't always
have the things u can
put your hands on

I Have Always Wanted a Woman To Be My Lover

How can it be morning in two places at once?
I was so happy when I moved into this house.
Finally a place where I can grow and hang my plants.
Finally a lover to love my difference and my sex;
her tongue discovering the secret parts of me.
I have always wanted a woman to be my lover.
How many men find this strange?
Once my father found his way to my bed.
He was not lost. I did not surrender.
I fought and was beaten and wet my bed with his blood.

Now a woman holds a knife to my throat
and I am speechless . . .

I did not know she would do such things.
How unnatural for a woman to beat another woman
after being lovers. Did she not whisper one night
when I was in her arms—no man would ever treat me
better?

My Father's Girlfriend

in
New York
my mother opens
her apartment door
after several knocks

her face
reminds me of Alberta
Hunter the year she
came out of retirement

in her eyes
something my father
fell in love with

How We Sleep On The Nights We Don't Make Love

One night
I looked into my parent's bedroom.
It was a night when I was home from college.
They were sleeping on opposite sides of the bed.
My father's arm almost touching the floor.
My mother snoring and shaking, one hand under her breast.
The room was dark but I could see how much older they had
become during my few months away.
They slept like strangers in a bus terminal or on a plane.
I refused to believe they were lovers.
I closed the door in order to keep their secrets.

Lover Behind a Blue Door

by the foot of the bed
a suitcase filled
with songs

on the chair a shirt
on the rug a shoe and
somewhere a sock laughing

he watched her sleep
face kissed by desire and
her back like a guitar

as he dressed
he thought of the words
he would one night sing
and one day forget

the moment when
she would awake and
see the blues eating
breakfast

the moment when he was gone

the space between notes
the door closing again and
again

did she go to new york city?

there can be nothing theoretical
about your woman leaving you
except the energy it takes to
control yourself which is perhaps
equal to the flood of tears
from both eyes
when the physical disappears
you wonder where the walls were
or maybe what kept you together
for so long
it's only natural that if you
open doors
one day you'll have to close
one
until then remember
love poems are written
for people who stare out windows
& always see Central Park

The Light On Rebecca's Breast

daylight falling on my chest
I place Jim's hands on the pillow
where my head embraced his love
I rise and enter the bathroom
where I wash with the door half closed
enough space to realize my life with
Jim is the reason I believe in miracles

I lace my sneakers after pulling
on a sweatshirt and running pants
a morning ritual when I celebrate
each new day as one of thanksgiving
and the counting of small blessings

the cancer will return
and I will not be able to out race it
or tell Jim that our lives are different
but just as beautiful
last night when he looked into my eyes
I could only confess my fear
just as now—I slip out for a morning
run through the woods while he
turns in our bed and his hands reach
for something he can no longer touch

Terrorism

my mother did not need terrorism
to feel unsafe in New York.
when I was a boy someone was always
getting stuck in the elevator. we
lived in the projects in the South
Bronx. this was before Soweto and
after Sharpsville. my mother first
believed the neighborhood was changing
when she could no longer obtain fresh
meat from the corner store.

Aaron

after watching
heston part the
red sea for the
first time
my brother ran
to his room
and pulled the
blanket from
his bed

he stood in the
doorway proudly
proclaiming
himself moses

he was the
oldest so what
he said was law
for my sister
and I

later that night
while my brother
slept I crawled
into his bed and
picked the lint
from his hair

Co-Star

my sister
a philosopher
in 1959
made this remark
in midtown Manhattan:

Why do all the beautiful
women have such ugly men?

The Boys of Summer

Carlton, Patrick and I
are waiting for autographs
outside Yankee Stadium. The summer
of 1960 and Mazeroski has not hit
the home run which will break our
hearts. We are years away from
memories, our wives and our children.
On this day we see Mickey Mantle coming
to work, his uniform of stripes waiting
inside. We run to catch "The Mick" to
have him sign his name on whatever we
own. Our lives sheltered from segregation.
Our mothers talking about Jackie Robinson
and how Willie Mays learned to catch a ball
while turning his back, running full speed
as if he were Emmett Till.

Players

When Mickey Mantle died
I saw myself once again
jumping against a fence
in the South Bronx, the
ball coming to rest in
my glove. My own centerfield
as large as the housing
projects so many could
not escape.

My Brother Richard Crosses the Street

one day my brother went to sleep and did not awake
my mother called me the next day
hysterical and several hundred miles away
what could I do but pack my bag and leave work early
I walked home because there was no rush to be somewhere
my brother was dead at forty-two and it made no sense
and I stopped at a corner waiting for the light to change
wondering what it felt like to cross the street into heaven

My mother and I are at the train
station. She is returning to New
York. We are early so I leave her
sitting on a bench alone. I walk
over to where the telephones are
and strike the pose of a movie
star waiting to kiss a lover good-bye.
I don't smoke so I have no cigarette
to dangle from my hands or lips. I
stare at my mother sitting on the
bench. She is talking to herself. I
think how crazy she looks. She clutches
her pocketbook fearful of strangers. She
looks at me with eyes that forget I am
her son. It has always been this way.
One of us going somewhere without
the other.

My Father Is Washing His Face

My father is washing his face
I listen to the water splashing in the sink
He rubs his hands together with soap
It is always Ivory Soap that makes his beard white
My father looks young for his age
This is something people always mention
when they see him
especially relatives who gather at funerals
and weddings
My father's face is a reminder
of what it means to be young
I am happy when someone says
I look like my father or when my
father reminds me to wash my face
and I reach for the soap in his hand

Bread

your father's skin
was soft like butter
my mother tells me
after grace

the two of us sit
at the kitchen table
where he once sat

our food cools
and we count
our blessings

share the bread
between us

The Gray Smoke of Clubs

I live my father's life
the absence of joy in the
center of responsibilities
the dark streets of early mornings
when he finds his way home
to a life already lost

In his bible the true meaning
of things unseen
Jesus is the comforter to an old
man who listens faithfully to jazz

I too hear the trumpet player's cry
the loneliness of his solo
My own life haunted by
the strange music of family
and the gray smoke of clubs

The night before the first
day of school

the night before the first
day of school. the house as
quiet as when I lived alone.
the cool summer air ending
as I breathe in the night.
during these moments of
fatherhood I count my black
blessings. I leave this poem
on the table next to the
lunch bags and books.

When We Are Alone

I let the children
climb into my bed. They
are afraid to sleep alone.
It is dark and they cannot
see. I feel their small bodies
against mine. A foot pushes into
the center of my chest. I tickle
it and it moves away to join a
silly laugh.

Tonight is a night for stories
and tales filled with monsters
and those funny space things. I tell
my children to hush and listen.

The stories begin
when we are alone and afraid
of the dark. We need the stories
to hold us. We need the words to
keep us warm.

Inheritance

(for Jasmine)

one week before June
my daughter tells me

she no longer wants
to live

her words
are my own

her sadness
deep

why this?

why this scar
on her soul?

why this
inheritance?

Science

When you were in elementary school
no one told you about the black laws
of cause and effect. Your science teacher
failed to teach you about why a police
club struck against a black man's head
in the south results in a house burning
down in the north or how prejudice can
make a store clerk's smile turn into a
coldness below freezing. You often
wonder while waiting in line how you
can become invisible to every atom in
the world. You try to understand the
reason for your condition. All the blues
you know cannot defy gravity. All the
jazz you hear cannot keep you from
exploding like a star.

Sidewinder, 1972

Lee Morgan dead and my roommate
decides he can't wait for graduation.
Packing his horn and clothes, he tells
me to keep the books. School is out.
Music has a gun to his head. I try to
tell him jazz is just another woman
with beautiful legs.

My Mother Wants To Be Young Again

after asking about the kids
for the second time
in our conversation
my mother tells me
aunt gwen died
I don't remember her I say
and it's true
I can't place a name with a face
or find a face for a name—
i've been gone too long
from the city
from my roots
from my parents
from the bronx and brooklyn
from the hudson and harlem
from myself and my mother
who asks again about the kids—
and I realize in her voice
she is telling me
she is afraid
afraid of cold apartments
afraid of snow and ice
afraid of stuck elevators
afraid of strange noises next door
afraid of who is opening her mail
afraid of the telephone
afraid of the dark
afraid of living alone
and waiting for death to visit—

my mother asks about the kids
and I tell her everyone is fine
I tell her a lie
because the truth is no longer gentle
the truth is no longer soft
the truth is no longer quiet
the truth is no longer
what my mother wants to hear—
my mother
wants the world to be young again
my mother wants to be young again
my mother wants to dance
my mother wants her hair to shine
my mother wants to play the piano
my mother wanted my father to say
I love you
my mother wants the music to live
my mother wants the music to breathe
my mother can hear the music
in the stories my kids tell
when they say hello to grandma
when they hold the phone with one hand
when they say daddy doesn't grandma get lonely
and can she come to visit—
when they say this
when they hand the phone back to me
when they run off to play
when it is just me and my mother
talking on the phone
no one listens to the silence
we hold each other with—
we can only hear our hearts
we can only say good-bye

we can only remember these moments
when we talk about the kids
and seldom ourselves—

and what would we say
after all these years
mother to son
son to mother—
how did we grow so far apart
how do we measure this distance
how far is it from you to me
how far from me to you—
this kiss is like a poem
this poem a kiss

Family Secrets

in a cabinet near the kitchen
she keeps her good silverware
the special things for company and holidays
cloth napkins folded in a manner
only her daughter will learn

she is a woman of secrets
a lady of whispers and promises
when she was young
she almost gave her child away

Father's Day

My wife asks
"What's wrong with you again?"

Her words cannot subtract the days
Or nights I have spent looking at her back
Or explain how a year's supply of loving
Is suppose to fit inside a Father's Day card

My son looks at me like a pitcher
Shaking off a sign and wanting to throw the
Hard fast one as he refuses to clean his room
Or take the garbage out

My daughter is long gone
Her body chasing some boy's smile around the corner
And I have grown accustomed to long moments of silence
I seldom answer the telephone or read the mail

But today a letter came from a friend in another city
She wrote to tell me about her garden
And how things are going so well this spring
She reminded me to water my heart

To let love grow through the weeds

Angela

I was too young to do the lord's work
so they left me by the side the road
and went walking off into the sunset
the shade of the car and the heat from
my own breath stuck on my tongue
like the words from the good book

They had a callin'
first my momma and then my daddy
someone called out their names
telling them there were things to be done
and this was the time for miracles to be believed

My daddy took the rifle from the basement
and I watched him bless it at the dinner table
telling my momma that this here should be the
tool they should give thanks for

I was five years old and could not reach
the butter or the bread and my momma asked
my daddy if this was the right thing to do

I still remember the silent look
he gave her and Jeff down the road gets
that look every time he sees a stray dog
so I know it's best for my momma to say amen
if she don't want an argument and to simply
trust in the Lord and in my daddy's house
the Lord wears blue underwear and watches tv

And I ask my momma to pass the bread
and daddy he put the gun down in the chair
next to me like it was my brother or sister and
it sat next to me while I ate and all the time
I kept asking myself why and when

we gonna go on a trip to the mountains
and give ourselves to the Lord my daddy finally say
he belch it out like he finished his food
but his plate still has meat and gravy on it

We gonna go to the mountains
and give ourselves to the Lord this evening
the world don't need us here no more
he ask my momma to fetch the bibles
and I say I'll help since we have bibles everywhere
where other folks have clothes and furniture we have bibles
hundreds of them

And my momma always tells me to trust in the good book
and I wonder which one
but this evening it don't matter cause
I'm scared and don't know what I believe
and when my daddy says he's ready to kill himself
let's go

I fall down on my knees and start crying
I can't pray to the Lord cause the Lord
done blessed my daddy and besides
I'm just a child and who would listen to me
and that's when my daddy said to my momma—
maybe she ain't ready to do the Lord's work
what you think?

And my momma looked at me like she was standing
over me in the bathtub studying me close
looking for some spot of dirt that I missed
and she pause and says softly
maybe she ain't ready
no— I don't think she's ready yet

Which is why they left me here by the side of the road
by the car with a box of bibles
and I watched my daddy lead my momma
towards the mountain
one hand on her shoulder and the other on his gun
and I don't know how far they got before they disappeared
cause I was crying like a lost sheep or maybe a stray dog
one that Jeff could find
I prayed for Jeff to find me cause I believed
the Lord already knew where I was

Houston
Christmas Eve 1954

Big Mama Thornton
sitting backstage
with Johnny Ace
nothing to do
but sing the blues
and put a gun to
your head

From the Letters of Brerbert

Now you know I always brings my own guitar. The music I have to look for . . . now this place Africa you talkin about seems like it was close to Mississippi and not Beaufort but then my memory comes and goes. Folks tend to be just a shade too light to be colored in parts of South Carolina. That's why so many rumors spread. Folks don't know who they talkin to. Now me—I keeps my mouth shut and I play. I let's my fingers tell the tale. Last time I heard my grandma hummin in the kitchen she was singin something that sounded African or maybe it was just a moan cause her feet hurt. I don't know but she always told me to add a little pork to the greens . . . maybe she was talkin about the music and I got the two confused . . . lately the music does sound sweet. Don't it?

From the Letters of Brerbert

Maybe I've been here too long. Snakes just get in my way, crossing my road with no legs. I'm a gator man. I went to Cuba when that Negro poet Langston went down the Mississippi. You remember he wrote that poem about the river and said it was for that DuBois fellow and not Booker T. Me and Langston saw a few snakes when that girl Zora was in town. She wanted to take a few to Harlem and dance some other dance. No it wasn't the funky chicken. It was pure Ellington. What you say about jazz? Sometimes you can find the pure stuff in them swamps. Strong blues mixed with rice and peas. You can't even get it in Africa . . . which is why I'm gonna stay here. I like the music and the land. Some of the people ain't too bad. So you tell Bertha she won't be seeing me -oh- and tell that hoodoo woman in New Orleans to see me if she wants her hair back. She's the one who invented the cake walk . . . sold it to the colored baseball league long before that boy Jackie learned how to hit and steal. Bertha is an old Dodger fan ain't she? It takes more than wine to live free and dream.

1907: Jazz in New Orleans

they say
Buddy Bolden
must be crazy

but his
music keeps
me sane

The Voice of Aretha Franklin Surprises Me

In Riyadh the wind blows the last prayer
beyond the veil of this city. In the Hotel
Al Khozama, I reach across the bed and
find the radio. The voice of Aretha Franklin
surprises me. I lie in the dark listening to
black music. I think of Baldwin playing
Bessie Smith in Europe and discovering
himself inside every note.

Roy Campanella: January, 1958

Night as dark as the inside
of a catcher's mitt
There are blows I can take
head on and never step back
from. When Jackie made the news
I knew I would have a chance
to play ball in the majors.
Ten years ago I put the number
39 on my back and tonight God
tries to steal home.

You Send Me: Bertha Franklin, December 11, 1964

What am I suppose to do
when the Devil comes knocking?
I pray to Jesus for protection
but I keep a gun like a blanket
for cold air and strange men.

Folks say I shot Sam Cooke
tonight but it was an angry man
I killed. I didn't hear any music
when he died, just the screams of
a young woman running from the
room next door. Her hands holding
the pants of love.

Nasrin

Where is my voice?
I can no longer write
with a veil over my words.
This silence is not prayer.
Is my talent gift or curse?
How do I celebrate my sex
without offending my God?
Inside the garden of my country
I am Eve afraid of Adam.

Elizabeth Alexander

I like to say your
name because it sounds
like an era or period
in time when kingdoms
were won or lost

your name a place
where rumors turn to gold
where love is buried
beneath desire

Yona Catches a Cab

we are so silly
laughing all the time
shaking our heads
and never giving up
on the world

we are simply colored

knowing our place
is where friendship
never ends

Tyson's Corner

The bell rings
and my jail cell opens.
I'm lean and mean and
back to box.

No lady is gonna
take me down
this time.

I can read better
now and write my
name (on your face).

Don't kid yourself
fighting ain't for
suckers or sweethearts.

Don't climb into my ring.
Don't knock on my door
at night.

Running With The Bulls

Morning conversations
coffee and tea
bagels with cream cheese
pastries as sweet as the plays
from last night's game

Smokers leaning against
the walls of downtown buildings
talking about the final score
and how Michael Jordan
did it again

We shake our heads and high five
laugh over our shoulders and
make our way to lockers
counters and desks

Once again we have faced
the morning traffic
defeated fellow workers for
parking space and looked beyond
the vacant stares of homeless men

We are running with the bulls
weaving pass outstretched hands
asking for nickels
dimes and daily grace

Carmen and the Fire Across Town

My father stood outside watching the fire burn, smoke swirling around his head. The crowd reminded him of church. Funerals. Families crying. My father once told me the world was changing. He did not care for change. He said it was cruel and crippling. My father was not a happy man. The death of his son left him covered with ash. A man on fire, forced to burn, to consume suffering. A black candle standing upright trying to provide light for a wife and daughter. Bodies trapped in the smoke of a small apartment. My father went out to look at a fire one day. He never came back.

I've Been Waiting For a letter From You

The wind blows a newspaper down the street
Four boys bounce a ball on the gray sidewalk
It's Friday afternoon and school is out
The mailman stops and opens the mailbox
I've been waiting for a letter from you
Here comes Maggie Anderson from the store
Her husband is still looking for a job
Late tonight they will drink and love and fight
It was that way before you went away
The sky is dark the rain is coming down
I close my window and pull down my shade
The bed in my room cries itself to sleep

A Painting of a Street In Black And Blue

I can feel the summer nights growing cold
The brown leaves falling to the ground from trees
A man walks his dog to the corner store
I watch it bark and jump and fight its leash
Across the street a small boy begs for change
His mother bends and wipes his mouth with love
On the stoop two old men share wine and smoke
Police drive by in their black and white cars
In the above apartment a blues crime
A young man moaning for a woman gone

A House In Provincetown

where the two streets meet
there is a house where our hands first met
and behind the house there is the water as
beautiful as when I first looked into your eyes
and wanted to swim naked into the rest of you

I remember the snow falling outside
as early as the first days of february
and we found warmth on the floor and I
rested on my back and felt the soft feet of
your hair walk across my chest

This Is Better Than a Letter From France

A black soldier returns home from the war
From the window his mother thanks the Lord
His little brother laughs and hugs him home
This is better than a letter from France
I listen to the radio and news
No one talks about the war in the South
In the moonlight the trenches look the same
I watch the soldier looking for his girl
Here she comes racing down the steps to him
Who cares if death is around the corner
Everyone will be in church on Sunday
I need to find a new tie for my suit
The soldier throws his hat to a neighbor
I watch it fall peacefully to the ground

The Inheritance of Islands

One night you try to
remember your father's face
unsuccessful you ride a dream
back into your mother's heart

In a small desk drawer
the confusion of letters and pictures
the stamps more attractive than the
handwriting on each envelope

This is your inheritance
your father's last glance
over his
shoulder

When you are older you will leave
and your mother will place your
first letters in a separate
drawer

She will close the door to another
empty room and walk outside to
her garden and watch the sunset
in the distant horizon

The water everywhere still blue

in small town usa

in small town usa
it doesn't matter if you can count
all the black people on one hand
and have a finger for yourself
it's 7 am and you look out the window
of your hotel and there's an old black
woman coming to work to scrub and clean
and this woman reminds you of your mother
tired but getting to work early and on time
never late as you close the curtain
and climb back into bed knowing you are
not alone and this woman is nearby
getting things ready for you and when you
leave your room you make your bed
and fold your towels hoping in this
small way to make it easier for this
woman you now pass in the hall
and you both wonder who will speak first
during this moment when being black is
all there is

Mountain Wife

in the yard
the truck sits stuck in mud
the hood bleeding from the last accident
I tell Carrie not to play near her daddy
not when he drunk or can't find work
I yell at her but she can't hear
ears deaf from my own screams
I wash our clothes with my tears
the hardness of my hand like his
I pass the mirror in the bedroom
and I recognize my mother's face
my husband sleeping in his clothes
just like my daddy did and now I dry
between my legs while praying
his spit won't make me pregnant

Letter from Carol

Carol's letter arrives today with two other pieces of mail:
a card inviting me to an art exhibit in Virginia
a second notice to renew my subscription to the *Nation*.

I open Carol's letter which is handwritten and two pages long.
It begins with her apology for not writing and is followed with
a short explanation

Carol has just moved to Chicago from Knoxville.
A migration she has made as suddenly and as quiet
as our first meeting last summer in Vermont.

She reminded me of my friend Lee
who came down from the mountains and took a lady lover.
And this is where the coincidence becomes a whisper . . .

Carol is getting married and her lover is a woman and
she tells me this as if she was describing her fiction or poetry.

The mail comes daily and I am grateful for these small moments
of communion and grace when letters are opened and sorted,
when stamps are saved and envelopes discarded.

I think of Carol and how our friendship was born out of hunger
and perhaps need. This too reminds me of love.

The Women

Ah Beautiful you are, my love, beautiful you are.

—The Song of Solomon 1:15

I.

My braids are extensions of my mother's hands.
The roots of my hair are my beginnings.

II.

My sister is my best friend, my best friend is my sister.
We hold hands, we embrace, we kiss.
We are sisters and so is our love.

III.

When I see myself I dance.

IV.

I will never lose my beauty.
The wrinkles in my skin are the rivers of life.

Is It Raining In Medford?

in a local newspaper
I discover the photographs
of two missing gay women

the airport is small
and so is the airplane
for which I have a ticket

the weather has never
been this bad for this
time of year

there are trees men will
cut down no matter what
it has nothing to do with

the side of the road
the rain falls

The Hands of Che Guevara

Outside Bolivia
the poor people of the world wait
for the ghost with no hands

In the hills and countryside
we continue to work for things
which remain invisible

Near Vallegrande
a door opens to a small church
revealing a wooden cross

Flowers & Nike Plants

I.

No water
No break

just my hair falling down my back
collapsing from the heat like when
my first child was born

forget about the pain and push
keep pushing

II.

How can a man fly without wings?
How can a man fly with shoes made by my hands?

III.

I curse the factory the way my grandmother cursed the war
and the first soldiers she saw with guns

She cursed their presence in the dreams of rice

My grandmother whispered to me the words of resistance
while I was in my mother's womb

What is the meaning of life?

IV.

Dear Buddha
here are my prayers
my candles and incense

let smoke
mix with clouds

let flowers reach
touching earth and sky

V.

I dream of nothing but sleep
my job terrible but real

hands
back
feet

hurting like water spilling from a jar

VI.

Last night
a holy man returned
wearing Nikes

his robes the color of sunset and grief

my faith as barefoot
as the day I was born

Urban Zen

I.
my blood
in the street
on our block

II.
beer
bottles
covering
the
cement
grass

III.
car
alarm
ringing
who
hears?

IV.
two
quarters
in my pocket
spare change
for he who
asks

V.
on the bus
no room
still we
stop
for
more

VI.
card
board
instead
of glass
for a window

VII.
my
neighbor
moved
to
where?

Orphan in Beirut

yesterday
I had a mother and father

yesterday
I had two arms

black boys

young black boys
sitting with their
backs against a wall
sneakers sparkling
while others stand
with hands pushed
deep into jeans
pants resting on
their hips as casual
as gunfire

Choirboy With a Horn
(for Michael Weaver)

I was a choirboy until
her love made me holy

sweet mass
dear father

the streets are filled
with disciples selling
heaven and needles

Charlie Parker blows his horn
and the walls of my church
crumble

jazz in her hair
and our bed unmade

I tried to kick the habit
and fight the sweetness
of her tongue

love kills and my lady loves
in a mysterious way

I was a choirboy until my altar fell
and the blues came down

Sponge

on the corner we called him sponge
because he didn't bleed like many
of us who were shot several times
and died too young to brag to show
the healed flesh wounds on basketball
courts in summertime or to girls
whose bodies covered ours on hot nights
and voices slipped and fell with each
breeze from one house to another

sponge shot twice in the alley with ellis
fell down and saw his hands absorb
the blood of his brother like a straw
this was something that made us believe
in jesus and others mention how farrakhan
was last seen being lifted up by a spaceship

in our school books we searched for the
first pages of this new testament

OJ Remembers Buffalo

yes
this is the curse
for once playing for
the Bills

like the agony
of Thurman Thomas
looking for his missing
helmet . . .

Sky

where is my hat?

the cold on my head
like another man's hair
standing straight
up on my back

in front the store
my hand opens to
strangers

only
a few coins in my
pockets

I need the butt
of a cigarette
to measure this
morning fog

Who would do such a thing?

The church among black people has been a social
cosmos; it has provided an emotional outlet, a
veritable safety value for people caught up in
the whirling storms of life.

—Kelly Miller

I.

the last few hours
I smell smoke around the evening
and I ask Mabel what's burning
and she says to check out back
and I look and nothing but the smell
gets in my eyes thicker than what I
smelled inside my house
where it comes from we don't know
but then the phone rings and Frank
Foster says it's the church and so
Mabel and I run out without our coats
not because it's warm but because we
just live down the street from where
we pray and God is our neighbor just
as much as anyone else

II.

anybody burn a church
ain't fit for forgiveness
who would do such a thing
we stand behind the firemen
and flames and see our prayers
disappear like dreams
the night air wraps the little ones

and we hold them against our hips and chests
and our arms are too short tonight to reach
out to anyone white and even the firemen
know water will only do so much
this town is caught in history like a child
trying to get a shoe off and the knot is tied
too tight

III.

ever since I've been here
black and white seem to get along
no trouble and no reason to expect
anything outside the norm like
a few folks not liking to be around colored
but then we keep to ourselves anyway
and I speak when I'm spoken to and I speak
when I got something to say and biting my lip ain't
how I was raised but never mine about me
Reverend Mackey talked with authorities
yesterday and they said they working on
solving just about every fire in the state
even though we ain't had nothing nearby catch
fire since old man Jeter fell asleep smoking
after making love to that young girl who said
she was from Chicago

IV.

I remember that night
Jeter half dress freezing outside his
own house and the fire not keeping him warm
but then stories like that make you laugh
and you take them as life's lessons and the
Lord working in mysterious ways
or the way Mabel figures an old man should change
diapers when he young not when he alone

she said she was right behind Jeter in the drugstore
when he put his arm around that girl and called
her baby—
baby what she was Mabel said and I had to hear
about it all night long especially if she died
and I had ideas of doing the same thing Jeter did
don't let me turn over in my grave was the last
thing Mabel said before she fell asleep

V.

flames flying higher than promises
our church just another one gone
I can't cry and can't soften my heart much
this place was to be a rock in trouble times
maybe things are just as bad as
when they told us we were slaves
and that lash burned our backs

Lord I want to believe everything
has a purpose under heaven
but these fires keep reminding me
of the hell we're in

City

although we live in the same city
the news always reaches us late
it comes in the middle of conversations or
when turning the page of a paper
after sports we glance at obituaries

we read them like box scores
who won
who lost
who died from AIDS
whose lover is not mentioned among
the survivors

we are all victims
the living and the dead
we let our fears divide us
we let it infect our wounds
even in the same city
we let our silence speak too loudly
we let our friends die alone

Cats

rain falls
in Seattle
black and white cats stretch legs
and leap to dry window sills to
see in

Autumn

the bay
near Seattle
wears a sweater to bed
the legs of autumn cross the street
too soon

Fish &Chips

lovers
holding hands on
Pike Street near the market
the smell of fish and passion in
the air

does everybody live in New York
or am I the last cowboy?

(for Zoe)

I have
some unpublished work
an Amtrak ticket
if I make it to Philly

maybe some Quaker or a
free person of color
will help me

all the cool
people are writing novels
or going to the opera

I can't even find
the jazz stamps
in my neighborhood

ain't nothing
like the frontier
if you need to
discover the blues

I hear Tonto
went electric
after he lost
his mask

and baby
you want me
to come to Brooklyn?

Omar's House

most of my socks have holes in them
so when I get to omar's house
the first thing I hear
in my head is my momma's voice
talking about
you never know what might happen
to you when you go out the door
that's why you gotta have clean undies
and socks without holes

and i'm thinking about this when
I see all them shoes waiting by
the front door of omar's house
like the beginning of one of those
samurai movies

omar pushes me away from the door
while I balance on one leg trying to get
my shoes off and maybe get a chance
to twist my sock around so no one
notice the big hole
but then omar's daddy extends his hand
and says as salaam alaikum
and I just mumble something like i'm
happy to be here and I really don't know
where I am except I know that omar
is a muslim

the first one I ever met who
didn't wear a bowtie or try to sell
me a newspaper
omar looks like me except he has
hair you can comb quickly
my momma say don't be talking about

good hair and bad hair anymore because
that type of thinking is backwards
what's important is what's under your hair
and if you have a hat rack instead of a head
then it don't mean no never mine about what
kind of hair you have and as salaam alaikum
omar's daddy says again

so I smooth the top of my head and stand
up straight and look him in the eye
and he smiles and tells me to put my shoes down
so now i'm ready to enter omar's house
and the first thing I notice is the living room
don't have no furniture
no couch
no lamp
no coffee table
just some nice rugs
the kind you see in the street and nobody
buys because they're too expensive and if you
don't have a vacuum cleaner or you have a dog
or cat there will be no way for you to keep it clean
so it be best for you to just look at it and
think it's a magic rug and maybe one day you fly
away from all the garbage on the sidewalk and near
the curb

omar touch me on my arm so gentle you think he was a girl
he is a quiet boy and my momma says he different from the rest
he doesn't curse and everything he does
he does with his right hand and then his daddy says
it's time for prayer and I look at him confused
because what am I suppose to do
the last time my momma took me to church was easter sunday
and the only reason we went was because she
got herself a mink coat and she said
I want everyone to see what your daddy got me

so I don't remember too much about jesus or the crucifixion
only thing I know is that my momma was the
happiest momma alive when she walked down the
aisle and sat in the front row of sweet savior
of the regiment first congregational church
everyone nodded at my momma and she whispered to me
and said
every believer in the lord should dress well
god don't like no riffraff

I look at my socks and i'm about to die
omar says the holy quran is the book I should read
and why his house seems like church I don't know
all I know is that I like it here
the sweet smell of incense
the plants in the window
the soft music coming from the next room

you omar's friend his daddy asks
yes sir I say
i'm omar's friend from school
we in the same class and I live around the corner
and I never met a muslim before
not a real muslim
not in this neighborhood
no—and you ain't no a–rab
because my momma saw you in the supermarket
and she told my daddy you was black and nice
because you said excuse me in front of the vegetables
as you reached for a plastic bag
and in all her years of shopping
nobody ever said excuse me to my momma
especially on a saturday morning

Omar In School

sometimes my daddy argues with my momma
sometimes it's about rent
or why my shoes suddenly grew small

my momma tell me one thing
me daddy tell me something else
which is why I don't do too good in school
especially with math problems like
how long will it take you to get to cleveland
if you left the day after tomorrow and the
train only runs on the weekends and the bus
cost $21.00?

so how am I to figure if it's day or night?
my daddy tells me to just look out the window
and we don't have family in cleveland - anyway

I tell this to my teacher
and she thinks i'm a smartass
she don't say this
but I know what she's thinking

she's thinking
why can't I be like omar
omar says yes ma'am and no ma'am
I like omar but he doesn't know everything

just yesterday I ask omar about jesus
I ask omar
did jesus have a dog?

omar says
he don't know

I tell omar
you stupid
you don't know

how a man gonna walk on water with a cat?
so he must have dog
a dog be a real disciple

I don't know what my momma believes
she thinks i'm just foolish in the head
my daddy thinks omar is strange
boy too old for his face
he tells me
looks like he knows everything

no— I whisper to myself
omar doesn't know the train to cleveland
only runs on the weekends

Oh Nigeria!

I.

it's Wednesday and it's lunchtime
and i'm waiting for omar to
come around the corner with a bag
of sweet things and other goodies
my mother holds the record for
consecutive bad lunches packed
for kids

here it's Wednesday and i'm going
overboard from hard salami and cheese
and wet tuna fish and bread
why can't she get sweet rolls like omar's mom
and fill a thermos with good warm soup
i'm not even a soup boy but then omar
is always getting inside my head
and telling me stuff I never heard of . . .

just yesterday he tells ms. greenfield
that there were muslims in africa
and ms. greenfield she has the tape
in her hand trying to fix the black
history bulletin board because it's february
again and I know she wants to use it on
omar

ms. greenfield she's just learning
about the sahara herself and maybe
where egypt is and now omar
wants to talk about muslims in africa

oh
nigeria
I say

omar taught me to say that because
he doesn't like to use bad words
whenever something bad or strange
is about to happen
omar says

oh
nigeria

so I say it too
and it keeps my mouth clean

II.

so how come allah let us be slaves?
I ask omar on the way home from school
omar keeps walking but then he slows down
and says

my daddy said
only the africans who lost
their wings became slaves
all the others escaped

my daddy said
allah gave us wings
and the holy book but some of us
didn't believe and started to do
bad things
so we had to be punished

suddenly I think of ms. greenfield
a black woman
trying to teach 30 of us something
and getting no help

I think of her being punished
for no reason at all
just like those africans

someone threw ms. greenfield
into the bottom of a boat with
no books
no pencils
no erasers
no computers
no art supplies
and not enough desks

everyday there be a chain of us
around her making noise and laughing
and only omar paying attention
and he wants to talk about muslims

III.

so we come to the corner
where we both live
and omar looks at me and says

happy black history month
and i'll have bean soup tomorrow
see you later

I watch omar run up the stairs
to his house
his long muslim shirt hanging out
from beneath his coat
his shirt flapping in the wind
like a wing

omar's front door opens
and I say

oh nigeria
(under my breath)

I Am Black and the Trees Are Green

so you point
and say the woods are beautiful
like men standing on the shores
of Africa enjoying the sun on their skin
the white sand touching the water blue
the new slaves as invisible as conversation

Koan

Consider
how the
cotton
grows
without
the slave.

The Slave Stripped Bare By Her Master, Even

My torn dress falls from my shoulders.
I turn my head away from his hair as
his hands stumble across the darkness
of my skin. He mumbles words mixed with
the sounds of animals. I did not expect
another ghost to visit so soon. This one
is younger and so the pain is like a cut
made by a knife or star; a broken piece
of glass shooting down from the sky. Near
the table in this room is where his father
sits and works. I must not disturb anything
here. I have been told many times not to
touch or steal. Even now I refuse to cry
or scream. I place my hand on the head of
the young ghost. I let some of his hair
tie to my fingers. Tonight I will give
them to the old woman. She will sing and
tell me what the stones say. The old woman
once stripped bare by her master, even.

Freedom

after word spread
about emancipation
some of us went to
the end of the
plantation and looked
for our children to
return. freedom don't
mean much if you can't
put your arms around it.

Hughes In Reno, 1934

when langston hughes lived in reno
he lived outside the blues
surrounded by mountains
he saw the beauty of blackness
in the clear night air

dark night
the light of New York
slipping out of my hand
like my father's last breath
before his heart failed

I watch a young man
throwing books into the water
his fair skin younger than
the moon

we are on a boat
going to Africa

there is a halo of blues
around his shoulders

I turn and walk down
the steps to the small
cabin room

I leave the young man
with his sadness
stories and poems

I leave him with
the music of the sea

Memphis in September

(for Jerry Ward)

A man standing on a balcony can change
history as much as the Mississippi

I watch a woman carry a wooden cross
down the middle of Beale Street

The many faces of Elvis
in store windows

I walk down Union Street talking with a
friend about the distance to Arkansas

At the Peabody Hotel I purchase postcards
and stare at dead ducks

In the doorway of the National Bank of Commerce
three men sleep snoring as loud as the blues

. . . and then Mr. Dorsey wrote Precious Lord

Not even the blues can comfort me tonight
My love lies shaken
A halo of darkness around my heart
I ask the Lord why?
My wife and child gone without farewell
I wish sleep would stumble through the door
My soul requires a hymn
How strange to find my hands so still

Salat

poetry is prayer
light dancing inside words
five times a day
I try to write

step by step
I move towards the mihrab
I prepare to recite
what is in my heart

I recite your name

Oklahoma

wind inside my soul
leaping across the flat land
love swaying like trees

Post-Card from Geneva

you tell me about your vacation
how you miss me

how you remain
forever with love - susann

I am always amazed
how you say so much
in such little space

Love, Still Life and Other Items

(For Susann)

Flowers and apples somewhere on Greenwich.
I buy a New York Times from the grocery store
and a carton of orange juice for my mother.
It is early morning and I wonder if you are
sleeping or getting ready for work.
The way I stand waiting for the light to change
and for cars to pass has nothing to do with
love, only that I care for you deeply and who
ever said "if you can make it here you can make
it anywhere" was not talking about my heart or
the way water in a glass grows warm after being
held in your hands.

For June

if I had met you
in '60 or '61
I would have given
you Valentine cards
made out of construction
paper and cut into
apple shaped hearts

I would have handed
over my Willie Mays
and Warren Spahn
baseball cards
my best cat eye marble
even two Almond Joys
a Milky Way
and some Twinkies

baby—I would have
loved you

given you everything

all this
and more

Chalk

the women on the bus wore no stockings.
it was winter and their legs were covered
with a white layer of ash, almost like snow.
things were changing and I took this to be
another sign of change, a reason for so much
death during this time of trouble and despair.
for days the news remained the same and I took
to reading my bible. I felt older now and more
vulnerable. when I went to work or to the store
my back was bent, my head low, my eyes afraid
of strangers, even friends. I was alone and my
community had become a place of darkness, of shadows
of hopelessness and unexplainable occurrences. I took
to keeping a journal, a written record of the drought.
there were streets in the city where there were no
trees or grass or growing things. only a white dust
like chalk, a film, a layer of death covering the
blackness of my flesh and memories of who
we were and what I had become.

About the Author

E. Ethelbert Miller lives in Washington, D.C. He is the author of several collections of poems. Mr. Miller was awarded the 1995 O.B. Hardison Jr. Poetry Prize. In 1996, he received an honorary doctorate of literature from Emory & Henry College. His E-mail address is EMILLER698@aol.com.